BLOCKCHAIN

----- ✥✥✥ -----

(THE TECHNOLOGY BEHIND BITCOIN AND OTHER CRYPTOCURRENCIES)

Tim Mathis

© Copyright 2016 by From Hero To Zero - All rights reserved.

The follow eBook is reproduced below with the goal of providing information that is as accurate and reliable as possible. Regardless, purchasing this eBook can be seen as consent to the fact that both the publisher and the author of this book are in no way experts on the topics discussed within and that any recommendations or suggestions that are made herein are for entertainment purposes only. Professionals should be consulted as needed prior to undertaking any of the action endorsed herein.

This declaration is deemed fair and valid by both the American Bar Association and the Committee of Publishers Association and is legally binding throughout the United States.

Furthermore, the transmission, duplication or reproduction of any of the following work including specific information will be considered an illegal act irrespective of if it is done electronically or in print. This extends to creating a secondary or tertiary copy of the work or a recorded copy and is only allowed with express written consent from the Publisher. All additional right reserved.

The information in the following pages is broadly considered to be a truthful and accurate account of facts and as such any inattention, use or misuse of the information in question by the reader will render any resulting actions solely under their purview. There are no scenarios in which the publisher or the original author of this work can be in any fashion deemed liable for any hardship or damages that may befall them after undertaking information described herein.

Additionally, the information in the following pages is intended only for informational purposes and should thus be thought of as universal. As befitting its nature, it is presented without assurance regarding its prolonged validity or interim quality. Trademarks that are mentioned are done without written consent and can in no way be considered an endorsement from the trademark holder.

TABLE OF CONTENTS

INTRODUCTION 1

PART 1 3

    BLOCKCHAIN – WHAT IS IT? 3

    BENEFITS OF BLOCKCHAIN TECHNOLOGY 3

    THE FORMATION AND WORKING OF BLOCKS 10

    UNDERSTANDING THE BLOCKCHAIN TECHNOLOGY 11

    HOW DOES BLOCKCHAIN WORK? 12

    PROSPECTIVE USAGES FOR THE BLOCKCHAIN TECHNOLOGY 20

    BUSINESS TRANSFORMATION 31

PART 2 35

BITCOIN AND OTHER CRYPTOCURRENCIES 35

    WHAT IS BITCOIN?? 35

    WHAT IS CRYPTOCURRENCY? 36

    HOW DO CRYPTOCURRENCIES WORK? 36

    WHAT ARE THE MOST COMMON CRYPTOCURRENCIES? 37

    WHY WOULD YOU USE A CRYPTOCURRENCY? 45

    SMART CONTRACTS 46

    TYPES AND INSTANCES OF SMART CONTRACT 47

    BITCOIN AND BUSINESS 48

WHY START ACCEPTING BITCOINS? 50
WHAT IS BITCOIN MINING? 53
IS BITCOIN SECURE? 58

CONCLUSION 63

INTRODUCTION

Whether it is for your own business, your job or for a vested interest, this book offers you the ultimate guide on to get started with Blockchain and Bitcoin technology. With proven steps and strategies as pillars, the book also details the benefits of choosing Bitcoin.

Over the past couple of decades, the internet has grown bigger and closer to individual households and organizations through e-commerce, education, banking and so much more. The transformation from analogue to digital has been incredible, and it was obvious that digital money was not very far off. Starting life as an open source concept that was created by an unknown group of people, Bitcoin is a digital currency that is independent of third party platforms, thus offering users very high security.

The rising value of Bitcoin has resulted in a steady rise in the number of companies and businesses, who are listed later in this book, who now accept this digital money. The steady progress of this cryptocurrency necessitates thorough knowledge about it which is why this book is perfect; blending everything you need to know about Bitcoin and Blockchain into a simple yet detailed platform.

BLOCKCHAIN

This book brings you the exciting history, the technology and the working know-how of Bitcoin. Additionally the book also explains the concepts of Blockchain, cryptocurrency and Bitcoin mining, while simultaneously bringing to light the important challenges that are faced in the process.

Thanks again for downloading this book, and I welcome you to the future of international transactions!

PART 1

BLOCKCHAIN – WHAT IS IT?

Though Bitcoin is more familiar than Blockchain and the other cryptocurrencies there is still an underlying confusion in the technical understanding of the terms, leading some to believe that Bitcoin is the same thing as Blockchain. This is not true. In simple terms, Bitcoin is a digital currency whereas Blockchain is the underlying technology behind Bitcoin.

BENEFITS OF BLOCKCHAIN TECHNOLOGY

Let us delve into detail about the benefits of Blockchain technology.

1) Transparency

- Blockchain-based systems have improved transparency compared to existing record keeping and ledgers. Ledger changes are visible to everyone on the network and transactions can't be altered or deleted once they are entered into the Blockchain system.

- With existing record keeping, anyone could alter databases and hide the changes if they knew how. Non-

BLOCKCHAIN

transparency of ledgers has led to countless cases of fraud going undetected. Manipulation and unauthorized alteration of data were allowed because of this issue with transparency.

- Blockchain technology provides transparency and thus transaction visibility to all entities on the network. The majority of computers connected to the Blockchain must approve transactions or changes to the Blockchain, to prevent hidden and manipulated transactions.

- Since all changes are shown in almost real time, this process occurs as transactions are approved and added to the Blockchain. Stealing money or hiding company losses by manipulating entries in ledgers is much less likely to occur with a Blockchain-based distributed ledger.

- Migrating to a Blockchain system in different industries provides transparency across a wide range of areas. The status of the transfer in any financial transaction on the Blockchain network can be seen in real time, in contrast to today's system of not knowing the status of a transaction until it is completed.

Anything of value that is recorded on the Blockchain system has this level of transparency. The uses and benefits of transparency in Blockchain will be discussed in further chapters, where we'll look at different industries where Blockchain technology is being developed and the transparency this provides to customers and businesses compared to existing systems that are currently being used.

2) Removal of intermediaries

As discussed at the beginning of the book, most transactions today require intermediaries such as banks to provide trust and security for transactions.

An advantage of Blockchain technology over existing systems is the ability to remove intermediaries by allowing transactions to occur directly between entities instead of involving a third party.

Billions of people in the world that live in countries where they can't trust third-party intermediaries due to corrupt governments, high crime rates, poor regulation of companies, manual record keeping or limited legal options to pursue claims can benefit hugely by the non-existence of third parties.

Blockchains are particularly useful in these cases where the trust in the intermediaries doesn't exist and transacting directly with other entities is risky as well.

Trust and transparency with reduced risks involved in transactions, without the need for a third party to act as an intermediary are provided by Blockchain systems.

3) Decentralization

The perfect example to remove intermediaries while simultaneously increasing trust and transparency is the decentralization of a Blockchain database. Maintained on a single shared ledger, users do not have to give up control to a single institution when using a Blockchain system and

BLOCKCHAIN

this makes collaboration between parties faster and easier to manage.

Citing the example of a group of banks transferring assets between each other, in the current scenario each bank would maintain their own ledgers and transaction records separately. A Blockchain-based ledger only asks to reconcile transactions to one shared ledger that all banks would have access to and they would then share a consensus on the correct record of transactions.

For competitor companies that are working together as part of an industry group, the decentralized structure of the Blockchain network is an advantage. One is always wary about handing over data or collaborating on a database that is owned by a competitor. One party owning all the data where competitors are involved could lead to lengthy legal contracts and nondisclosure agreements for protecting the privacy and access of data. A Blockchain-based system eliminates this and enables competitors to work together and share a database with full access and control.

Prone to hacking, data loss and corruption, central databases are a big contrast to Blockchain where all computers on the Blockchain network have a copy of the Blockchain, reducing the risk of data loss and eliminating a single point of failure, manipulation or data corruption. To manipulate the data on a Blockchain network requires "hacking" over 50% of the computers on the network at the same time, which is almost completely impossible.

PART 1

4) Trust

The conventional methods for transacting between entities require a trusted intermediary to facilitate the process. The Blockchain system allows intermediaries to be removed while still maintaining trust and security between the transaction parties.

Blockchain networks are generally decentralized, with all people connected to the network having access to the Blockchain thus enforcing trust in the Blockchain network itself. The increase in trust between entities in a transaction is an important non-tangible benefit of decentralization and improved transparency of Blockchain.

5) Security

Blockchain provides immutable data that can't be altered or changed. Every block of data on the Blockchain network can also be traced back to the first "genesis block".

The immutability of data combined with the domino effect on the blocks in the Blockchain creates an easy to follow transaction audit trail.

History speaks of countless cases of fraud and data manipulation. The post-fraud trail is always altered making investigation difficult and time-consuming thus making it impossible to trace the transactions or fraud.

Transaction history can't be altered in a Blockchain based system, thus, leaving a clear trail of the events on the Blockchain. As already discussed, altering an existing transaction would require controlling over 50% of the computers on the network simultaneously, which is almost completely unfeasible. If this occurred, it would be quickly spotted by the network computers anyway.

The Blockchain solves many of the security issues in conventional systems, even though its security is not flawless and overrides the current system excellently. Though full elimination of fraud is impossible, the Blockchain provides a clear audit trail back to the start of a process allowing attempts at fraud to be easily identified.

6) Wide range of potential uses

While almost anything valuable can be recorded on the Blockchain, "valuable" doesn't necessarily mean of financial value. It can be a record of ownership, a digital identity, a copyright license, digital files or anything that could currently be recorded in a database.

Let's take the example of copyright licenses; these are assets of value, and the licenses are just data or numbers stored in a database. The value comes from what copyrights these licenses have and income derived from what the copyright protects.

The organizations that control and manage copyright licenses in a centralized database can be removed by storing these assets of value on the Blockchain. Assets of value such as cryptocurrencies, licenses and other digital assets can exist solely on the Blockchain system as native Blockchain assets making them easier to manage than existing records of ownership.

PART 1

Being easily accessible, especially with recent innovations such as the Ethereum platform and smart contracts, Blockchain allows anyone to develop applications that utilize its technology.

Having the potential to change almost every industry in the world, Blockchain-based systems are being developed by many companies which shows the impact it is having on everyday life.

7) Reduced costs

Cost reduction in many industries by removing intermediaries involved in the process of recording and transferring assets is done by Blockchain. Every intermediary or layer involved in a transaction that adds costs to recording, and transferring assets is the traditional manner is eliminated.

A distributed ledger allows parties to transfer assets on one shared ledger, reducing the costs of maintaining multiple ledgers in each organization; the latter being how the current systems function. Blockchain-based distributed ledgers provide real-time settlements and auditing from all connected parties for every transaction.

8) Increased transaction speed

The speed of transactions is also dramatically increased due to Blockchain-based systems. By removing intermediaries and settling transactions on a shared distributed ledger, Blockchain-based ledgers transactions are settled instantly.

BLOCKCHAIN

Currently, money transfer takes a few days to reflect in the receiver's account- similar to credit card purchases where transactions remain pending for several days. In line with these examples, Blockchain-based systems are being developed to increase the speed of these transactions. However this isn't limited to just these examples - any transaction or transfer of value could potentially use Blockchain technology to increase the speed of transactions.

Further on in this book, real-world examples of companies that are developing Blockchain-based systems to increase the speed of transactions will be discussed.

THE FORMATION AND WORKING OF BLOCKS

The Blockchain is made up of blocks, each of which holds a valid transaction. Each block includes a hash before it which links them together.

These links form the chain. In addition to a hash-based history, every Blockchain database also contains a specific algorithm. This is used to score different historical versions which enables choosing a version of higher value above others. Peers that support the Blockchain databases do not have access to the same version history all the time. Instead, they just hang onto the highest scoring version. When a peer gets a newer version with a higher score, it will automatically add a new block added to the chain. At this point the database that each block holds is overwritten, and an update is sent to the other peers. However there is absolutely no guarantee that an entry will stay in the database as the highest scoring version forever. Since a Blockchain is built to add the score of a new block to the total score of the existing blocks the probability of an entry being superseded is low, especially as more blocks are added, and there are certain incentives in this addition of new blocks compared to working with only old blocks.

UNDERSTANDING THE BLOCKCHAIN TECHNOLOGY

There is absolutely no doubt that the focus that was once only on a single cryptocurrency is now quickly moving towards applications that are based on cryptocurrency and that are built on a Blockchain. The technology of the Blockchain is almost the same as that of the database, barring the way we interact with them.

With the technology being new, the terminology used in understanding the block systems are not yet standardized. The simplest form, the block-chain, acts as a joint, replicated, added database where access to the record is shared, but verification is performed by all the participants. The most common elements across the chain systems are:

- A data warehouse, usually containing financial transactions or any other kind of data and which is responsible for replicating data across multiple systems in real time

- Hierarchical client-server models are replaced with a peer-to-peer network topology.

BLOCKCHAIN

- The increased use of cryptography and digital signatures to confirm the identity, authenticity and security of read/write rights and permissions.

- Mechanisms that make it difficult to modify historical records and easily detect unauthorized modifications.

- Though the locks differ in configuration, their main function is to check whether the network is publicly available or private.

- This differs from a private network. Blocking systems have different mechanisms and protocols and are classified as public or private based on whether one can write to them without needing additional permissions or if the participant pool is a limited one respectively. But blocking the circuit or making it private adversely affects the design of the system, which is why making it public is recommended. But locks that can be publicly written are much more limited than their private counterparts.

HOW DOES BLOCKCHAIN WORK?

The three principal technologies that make up the Blockchain are:

- Private Key Cryptography

- A distributed network with a shared ledger

- An incentive to service the network's transactions, maintaining records and security

PART 1

Though none of these technologies are new to the industry, using them together results in something awesome. How these technologies orchestrate together is what we will see next.

THE WORKING STAGES

- To be part of the Blockchain system, software needs to be installed by participating entities that run it to connect their computer or server to the network. By running this software participants act as separate validators, called network nodes.

- A node network manages a database, also known as a block-chain. Nodes are entry points for new data and are responsible for checking and distributing new data that has been sent to the Blockchain.

- But in a distributed system without a golden source of truth, the question is "how will the network come to a consensus as to what is to be written on the block? Without a boss for arbitration, how should a conflict be resolved?"

- The answer to this is through protocols. The block system will have a protocol; that is a set of pre-agreed rules for the technical and business validation of data to help with reaching a consensus.

- A block is created by grouping such transactions. These blocks are added in chronological order in a way that it resembles a chain - hence the name Blockchain. The new blocks are then stored in your local Blockchain databases either on your server or your workstation by the nodes.

BLOCKCHAIN

Let's delve into some more detailed terminologies:

CRYPTOGRAPHIC KEYS

- During a transaction over the Blockchain, a Public Key which is in the form of a hashed version is sent across by the two parties.

- The Private Key is the other type of key that is private only to the one who uses it, which means each entity in the network knows only its own private key.

- The sole purpose of the Private Key is to derive the Public Key.

- Both the Private and Public Keys are usually represented using the Wallet Import Format (WIF) which comprises of letters and numbers.

- Each Blockchain transaction from a sender requires a signature that is generated using a Private Key. Therefore Private Keys are used to sign the cryptocurrencies you send to others. Unless someone else has your Private Key, it is almost impossible to hack the code and make transactions in your place.

IDENTITY

- Private and Public Keys only authenticate a transaction and are not enough to secure digital relationships. There must be a mechanism to combine with the key structure for approving the transactions.

- A Distributed Network fits this requirement. It ensures storage of the transaction records by all entities in the Blockchain.

- In the event that a system gets hacked and data is altered, the others in the network are not very likely to get affected because of the distributed and decentralized nature of the network. Hacking such a network requires too much effort and innumerable resources that are not possible to attain.

- This means the security of the network is dependent on the size of the network, which is an appeasing characteristic of the Blockchain. Being superbly huge and requiring unimaginable computing power, it results in an impenetrable form of digital security in combination with cryptographic keys.

The Incentive

Ours is not a perfect world. No one is doing anyone any favors by securing the global network. It is also evident that such huge amounts of computing power will come at a cost. So the question is how do we attract investors to help with this?

Mining

- The solution is simple. For public Blockchains, a process called mining rewards relevant 'miners' with golden benefits and incentives as in the literal sense of the term.

BLOCKCHAIN

- With Blockchains, there is an incentive for offering your computer processing power to the network in addition to the person's vested interest in public service.

- Let us see how Bitcoin serves to be the incentive. Unique Bitcoins that provide value are considered here. This is made possible by the nodes serving the network creating and maintaining a history of transactions for each Bitcoin by solving mathematical problems.

- Voting with their CPU power, the miners agree or disagree with the new blocks or invalid blocks. The majority of the miners then arrive at the same solution, thus adding a new time-stamped block that may contain data or messages to the chain.

AN EXAMPLE OF A BITCOIN TRANSACTION

- Bill owns some Bitcoins. For inter-entity transfer, a digital signature will be produced on the statement by using the cryptographic keys by Bill to make a transaction.

- Next, Bill signs a statement on his own computer agreeing to transfer some coins to Jack without actually sending the statement across. It is clear that the coins have not been transferred out of his account. Therefore this will not be witnessed by anyone on the distributed network and cannot be considered as a legitimate transaction.

- Now even if Bill did send the signed statement to Jack, it will not be considered transacted if Bill has signed another transaction statement saying that he wants to

PART 1

transfer the coins to Hilda, which he only sends to Hilda. Bill will have effectively spent his coins twice only if Jack and Hilda both accept these statements that they have received the coins from Bill.

- Let us now see where the benefit of a distributed global ledger comes in. If Bill wants to transfer his coins to Jack, a statement authorizing the transfer must be published by him to the Blockchain. This will be authorized by the Blockchain maintaining Miners only if Bill has not yet transferred the coins to anybody else. Once Jack sees the transaction appear in the Blockchain, he knows that he is the new owner. Any other statement made by Bill further on saying that he has transferred the coins to Hilda will never be approved into the Blockchain because the transaction to Jack was published first.

THE MINING PROCESS:

1. Once a transaction block is created miners take the data from the block and apply a mathematical formula to it, turning it into a hash which can be any combination of alphanumeric characters. The block and the newly-generated hash are saved at that instant of time where the block terminates.

2. Hashes have some very interesting properties. Producing a hash from data like a Bitcoin block is not difficult, but it is impossible to figure out the hashed data only by viewing the hash. Each hash is unique even if the procedure to produce it is simple. Even a single character change results in a completely different hash.

though the chain.

3. A hash is generated by formulating together the transactions in a block with the hash of the last block stored in the Blockchain. This process enables the hash to act like a digital wax seal that confirms the chronology of every block in the chain and ensures that any tampering would be visible to every entity present. This way the domino effect is in the Blockchain, since any tampered-with hash would result in the hash of the next block being wrong, which would continue throughout the chain.

4. Faking a transaction by changing a block that has already been stored in the Blockchain would not work since that block's hash would totally change. If the block's authenticity is checked by a miner with the help of the hash function, the hash would be different from the one already stored alongside that block in the Blockchain. This would help to spot the fake block.

Competing for coins

Block mining requires software that is specifically written for this purpose. With Bitcoin, every time a hash is successfully created the respective miners are rewarded with 25 pieces of Bitcoins, subsequently updating the Blockchain and informing everyone on the network about it.

Since producing hashes with the help of computers is very easy, the Bitcoin network has to make it more challenging, or else it would lead to hundreds of transaction-blocks every second, and it would take merely minutes to mine all the Bitcoins. 'Proof of work' is introduced by the Bitcoin protocol, thus making it tougher.

Any random hash will not be accepted by this protocol. It has to adhere to a format. For instance, it must have a certain number of zeroes at the start. There is no way to guess what a hash might look like before it is produced, and as soon as a new piece of data intrudes in the mix, the hash will change to totally a different one.

The Data Miners do not meddle with the transaction data in a block, but they change the data they're using to create a different hash. A hash is created by a random piece of data called the nonce. The nonce will be changed, in case the hash cannot be fit with the format that is needed, and the hash will be created again. It can take multiple attempts to find a nonce that works, and all the miners in the network simultaneously work on this. The miner with the best computing power will have the highest chance to find the correct hash and hence it is best practice for miners to pool their computing power to find that hash.

HOW LONG DOES IT TAKE TO BUILD A BLOCK?

Since blocks are discovered by a random process there is no way of telling exactly how long it will take for a certain number of blocks to be chained, even though it is popularly believed that it takes an hour to build a community standard of six blocks. On average, it takes about 10 minutes to find each block. The difficulty of mining is directly proportional to the size of the blocks. However, the progress of mining speeds cannot be determined even with the latest technology and high amounts of computing power.

BLOCKCHAIN

PROSPECTIVE USAGES FOR THE BLOCKCHAIN TECHNOLOGY

Blockchain in Banking: a measured approach

The Blockchain is an emerging technology that has put the financial services industry at the brink of transformation by giving way to faster, cheaper, more secure and more transparent transactions. Let us lay down our thesis on how the market is shaping up and what financial institutions should consider as they move from innovation and research to pilot deployments.

In Summary

Blockchain, which is the root technology on which crypto-technologies such as Bitcoin are based on, is ready to solve many problems facing the banking industry - the history of the blockade being one of the unintended consequences. Originally created as a Bitcoin transaction tracking database, Blockchain is also known as a distributed book. Designed in 2009, it allows individuals and organizations to process decentralized transactions using sophisticated algorithms and a consensus to verify transactions. It has been seven years since its commencement and many startups, banks and financial players today rely on this amazing technology to provide a reliable alternative to systems that depend on intermediaries and third-party transaction verifications. Many people are using the distributed accounting method of Blockchain to create a system that decentralizes trust which is a radical departure from the existing transaction processing methods, and significantly reducing all types of transaction fees and processing time is their primary objective.

PART 1

Blockchain has unimaginable potential which can be compared to that of the early commercial Internet; the critical difference being that the Internet allows data exchange while Blockchain allows the exchange of value. It can allow users to trade around the world without the need of payment processors, custodians and organizations for settlement and reconciliation. Although Blockchain is positioned as an open system for processing transactions in the financial system, banks have internally experimented with a distributed register approach to create an efficient, single version of the digital truth. Automating processes, reducing data warehouse costs, minimal duplication of data and improved data security are some of their goals. Similar to Internet and e-commerce, an 'open-to-all' Blockchain that violates the traditional financial market can be linked with only a trial and error deployment within the scope of limited parameters, through internal tests and with associations between start-ups. However in order to realize the complete blocking potential in the financial system, unity and standardization in the banking industry is necessary to ensure compatibility.

Nevertheless, many fundamental questions loom before the banks that are planning to deploy the block-schemes. As an example, though existing systems are built on reliable and obsolete solutions, how does one determine the process that will move to the Blockchain? Additionally given the rapidly changing landscape of the blockhouse, developing a sound long-term plan of action that includes experiments, strategical deployments and scaling in a logical progression to ensure a successful transition from a centralized heritage to a fully distributed processing of digital transactions is critical.

BLOCKCHAIN

Vital considerations that can be useful to banks studying the Blockchain include:

- Enlisting innovative opportunities
- Feasibility and Impact studies on the existing system.
- Verifying the evidence of the concept
- Detailed study of the effects of information security
- Cut-off realization of the block chain: open or authorized
- Transaction scalability planning
- Building partnerships and cross-functional, inter-industry cooperation.

Blockchain's promise: Banking and Beyond

The digital cryptocurrency has become a subject of debate ever since the first Bitcoin transaction in January 2009. The technology of Blockchain and distributed book began to attract the attention of banks and start-ups by the end of 2013, though they had initially feared the concept.

Blockchain's method of checking and tracking transactions is what lured consumers to it. It relies on a consensus between a peer-to-peer network of computers based on complex algorithms, instead of a third-party or central bank. Instead of a single database, transaction blocks with timestamps are stored in all the value chain systems. This non-intermediary, decentralized mode of trust has given rise to opportunities for creating processes such as transboundary payments, resulting in faster, more reliable and cheaper trade and settlements.

Increased competition

Markets that are traditionally dominated by banks and other financial institutions can be accessed by Blockchain. In this digital age, banks are witnessing an increase in competition from non-bank players in fields of loans and mobility payments. There is a likelihood of an increase in competition, thus reducing the technological barriers for non-traditional supporters that are not digitally measurable.

Some examples include:

- Allowed block circuits: Companies can create blocked blocks that are designed to select customers for a specific purpose. Setl, which created a permit-based accounting system that can move money and assets in real time to calculate market transactions, offers this service.

- The creator of liquidity: Companies can become market-makers with a system based on blockages and open cash in exchange for completing a cross-border transaction at a lower rate which can, in turn, allow non-profit organizations to compete with banks.

- Equity financing: Smart contracts can be used by a block-based platform to give back funding for equity financing.

- Hybrid crediting: Companies can seek funding from peer-to-peer lenders based on the chain. With lower operating costs than traditional banks, such lenders charge lower interest rates. The DApp LoanCoin credit network is an example of hybrid lending.

These points are a huge incentive for banks to play around and make maximum benefits in these areas. Similar to non-traditional technological players, banks can create their own versions of these platforms on the block-chain and without compliance they can quickly infiltrate their traditional strongholds.

New Prospects in Banking

A new set of opportunities are assumed to be created by Blockchain for banks co-operating with start-ups to study the niche of business directions. These include:

Internet of Things (IoT) plus Blockchain: Offline transactions can be performed by enabling intelligent devices through intelligent contracts.

Tracking of health benefits: A Blockchain system can ensure that the nursing allowance is spent exclusively on health care activities, thus saving time spent on post-transaction reconciliation and helping with direct processing.

Any trade: The platform can allow an exchange for any underutilized asset (wireless routers, storage in computers, coupons, etc.), in exchange for a service or product already agreed upon.

PART 1

A Rush of Startups and Incumbents

Start-ups and operators, especially in the banking and finance domains, are the ones that best appreciate the appeal of Blockchain and its resulting applications. The primary reason is that the estimate sets the number of launches of blockades to more than 200, with an average estimate of $4.4 million USD. Venture capital financing for Bitcoin and Blockchain start-ups has reached $ 1 billion in 2015, and is expected to cost $ 2.5 billion by 2016.

By coordinating with start-ups or creating pioneering laboratories, many top Western and European banks are researching Blockchain applications to test their evidence of the concept. A ground-breaking concept is a consortium formed by blocking R3, which has, as of now, attracted 42 international financial institutions. A general laboratory block chain has been created by R3 for the financial system. Recently 11 partner banks were linked to a peer-to-peer distributed register, and industry standards and protocols were enforced to block banking transactions. Commercial applications for banks and financial institutions will also be developed. R3 efforts to create industry standards are a small but significant step towards creating interoperability solutions of Blockchain in the financial system. Banks and start-ups are more active in domains including cross-border payments, trading activities, storage services and customer-behaviour analysis.

For example, certain figures are listed below:

- Santander has identified 20-25 uses with regards to international payments and prudent contracts

25

BLOCKCHAIN

- Barclays is working on 45 experiments internally
- Citibank has its own version of Bitcoin called Citicoin
- Several new facilities were received in 2015 due to a sharp rise in non-financial start-ups.

This picture suggests that cases of non-financial use exceed those of financial uses, which indicates that real-world assets may increasingly be associated with blocking and trading.

The main elements of Blockchain include:

Decentralization: A common infrastructure is created by distribution control between all peers in the transaction chain, instead of a centralized approach to the ecosystem.

Digital Signature: The exchange of transaction value via digital signatures that are exclusive and are dependent on Public Keys (with a known decryption code) and Private Keys (codes are known only to the owner) to generate ownership confirmation is a prime feature of Blockchain.

Mining: Miners are rewarded by a distributed consensus system for verifying and validating transactions and saving them in blocks using strict cryptographic rules.

Data integrity: Complex algorithms and user consensus ensure that transaction data, once agreed, cannot be changed. This means the data stored in the Blockchain is the only version of truth for all entities involved, which reduces the risk of fraud.

Efficiency and cost reduction: Apart from trade promotion, the robust Blockchain model can also be applied to non-monetary transactions. By eliminating errors and duplication, Blockchain is ideal for converting a multitude of digital processes.

The main advantages of the Blockchain are:

- Calculation time is reduced to a few seconds without middlemen.

- Third parties are eliminated and instead, the participation of all entities in the value chain to cloud assets come together to verify the identity of each party.

- Measurable improvements in security, areas of payments and credit card fraud through a decentralized history of public transactions, which stores transaction data that is continuously checked by miners

- Material cost reduction by elimination of expensive private infrastructure

- Elimination of error handling through real-time transaction tracking

- Full automated transaction processes, from payment through to settlement

- Removal of network bottlenecks caused by duplication

- Risk reduction due to data integrity is ensured by the chronological storage of data enhanced by cryptography. This, in turn, reduces the burden on compliance and reduces the cost of regulation in areas such as knowledge of your customers (KYC)

BLOCKCHAIN

Implementing Blockchain

Although there has been increased activity over the past year, it is still very early for the blockade. Banks have started initiating Blockchain and are at varied stages of internal testing. The functioning of banks radically changes when Blockchain causes changes such as storing data in several places, rather than in one central location. In terms of organizational culture, this can become a serious obstacle to overcome. It would be unreasonable, therefore, for banks to not start taking steps to incorporate the blockade into their existing systems.

It is best that banks follow the best practices listed below when implementing the Blockchain platform together with existing systems.

Lookout for innovative opportunities: Blockchain is a common database, and banks typically use database management technologies. Hence the pre-pilot primary question is "which are the processes that need to be moved to the block chain?"

Data access control: A perfect place to start would be the creation of a working group that explores the pros and cons of moving a process to a block. Functioning as a start-up, it will explore areas where a Blockchain can add value while still in line with the bank's strategic goals.

Feasibility and Impact Study on existing systems: Weighing the benefits and costs of moving the process for blocking is vital.

The influence of key stakeholders and partners

Test the proof of concept: Though testing can't begin in the initial phase, it needs to be done once the proof-of-concept (PoC) application is ready against real-world simulations to identify areas of improvement. Banks will thus be able to fine-tune the application and use this knowledge to develop future applications by measuring the results against expectations.

Data security and regulations: Laws are important in the implementation of the Blockchain. There are no known provisions in the current regulatory framework on the use of technology to eliminate intermediaries. Data privacy laws that may vary from country to country need to be complied with when saving customer data on computers in different countries. Also, a rule-framework for allowing contracts on today's capital markets does not exist. Introducing this factor in the early stages of development is safer in the long-term, even though there will be an eventual development of regulators.

Open or Allowed Blockchain Implementation: Most of the banks are working on closed / allowed blocking platforms. Since the technology is in its embryonic stage maintaining control is reasonable, meaning that the central administrator authorizes participation in the Blockchain. Reduction in transaction costs, which is a major advantage of decentralization, cannot be achieved without giving up control. This block-chain approach makes sense in the short term, but as the platforms come out on their own then industry players will realize the real benefits of the Blockchain platform.

BLOCKCHAIN

Scalability calculation: The Bitcoin community continuously improves Blockchain to increase the processing efficiency of transaction processing from the chain of blocks from the current limit of seven transactions. In reality banks process thousands of transactions per second, which is huge. The proposed solutions include increasing the block size limit from the current 1 MB per block, introducing direct payments channels between two users and implementing centralized servers that process transactions with an indirect chain.

Looking forward: Partnership and Cooperation. Designing plans that allow Blockchain technologies to coexist with their inherent systems is a priority action item for banks. The "wait and see" approach is believed to be suboptimal out of all other Blockchain approaches. In order to replace the current banking systems, more maturity and increased reliability is necessary for the product. Potential obstructions can be averted in the long term with a protocol that ensures interoperability. Since this still needs to be conceived, banks that are starting to migrate their processes to Blockchain should begin by gauging how interoperability can improve their chain goals.

It is time to begin, and to this end banks are inclined to use the approach that combines internal testing with group participation, including using related banks and technology providers to investigate the use of the chain. These experiments will lay the groundwork in the form of protocols and standards on which the future of the block chain resides. Technology Leaders such as R3, Hyperledger Project, Post Trade Distributed Ledger (PTDL) and Digital Asset Holding create a safe space for conducting pilot tests for prototype blocks. Financial institutions and technology providers can

PART 1

feed on each other's ideas and experiments while concurrently researching action-items and pain-points. Banks can then identify and create key skills and use collective knowledge to design a plan that will facilitate a smooth and inevitable transition to an awesome chain-based future.

BUSINESS TRANSFORMATION

Budgetary Services

Custom frameworks tend to be bulky, error-laden and infuriatingly moderate. Go-betweens are frequently expected to intervene in the procedure and resolve clashes, which causes stress and costs time and money. In contrast Blockchain is cheaper, straightforward and more compelling. Shrewd securities and keen contracts are utilizing this framework to pay advances. The former consequently pays bondholders their coupons once certain prearranged terms are met. The latter is computerized and gets that done with self-executing and self-keeping up on the meeting of conditions.

CASES OF BLOCKCHAIN MONETARY ADMINISTRATIONS

Asset Management: Trade Processing and Settlement

Resource administrations (where parties exchange and oversee resources) have conventional exchange forms that can be costly and unsafe, primarily with regards to cross-fringe exchanges. Each group; i.e. agent, overseer, and the settlement administrator simultaneously keeps their own records, thus increasing waste and inviting blunders. By encoding the

31

records the Blockchain record reduces mistakes, streamlines the procedure and wipes out the requirement for middlemen.

Insurance: Claims preparing

Preparing cases can be baffling and difficult. Processors that are coded for protecting frauds need to look through fake cases, divided information sources and relinquished arrangements for clients to express and prepare these structures physically – giving a massive chance for errors to occur. The Blockchain gives a straightforward and ideal framework free administration. Its encryption enables safety net providers to take the responsibility of being safeguarded.

Payments: Cross-Border Payments

Globally the instalments domain is expensive, prone to mistakes and open to illegal tax avoiders. Cash takes days, if not longer, to cross the world. The Blockchain is now teaming up with settlement organizations like Abra, Align Commerce and Bitspark that offer end-to-end Blockchain fueled settlement administrations. In 2004, Santander became one of the primary banks to combine Blockchain with an instalments application, empowering clients to make worldwide instalments 24 hours a day with next day clearance.

Shrewd Property

Licenses, property titles and organization shares, which are unmistakable or immaterial properties, can have shrewd innovation implanted in them. Such an enrollment can be put away on the record with authoritative subtle elements of other people who are permitted proprietorship of this property. The allowed party can gain access by using savvy keys after which

PART 1

the record stores and permits the trading of these keys on confirmation of the agreement.

A framework that can be used for recording and overseeing property rights is created by the decentralized record, and additionally can be used in allowing the shrewd contracts to be copied if the records or the savvy key is lost.

Marking the property as a 'keen' one helps to reduce the rate of extortion, find mediation expenses and find erroneous businesses, simultaneously boosting trust and proficiency.

Cases of Blockchain Smart Property

Unconventional cash loan specialists/hard cash loaning

The conventional loaning framework can be reformed by brilliant contracts. For example, borrowers with poor credit and advance requirements can benefit from eccentric cash banks (e.g. hard cash banks) and are charged 2 to 10% of the advance sum in addition to giving their property as security. This leads to borrowers facing liquidation issues and losing their homes. This is undermined by Blockchain, which can enable an outsider to credit you with cash and take your property as security without having any reason to demonstrate any loan specialist credit, work history or physically handle varied reports. Blockchain has the property encoded publicly.

Your auto/cell phone

Brilliant property has primitive types as well. As an example your car might have an immobilizer, where the auto is initiated once you tap the correct key convention. Your cell phone too

BLOCKCHAIN

will follow suit once you write in the correct PIN code, proving to your phone that it's your property.

Primitive types of shrewd property have the drawback of holding the key in a physical compartment; the auto key or SIM card, for example, can't be exchanged or duplicated. The Blockchain record tackles this issue by enabling Blockchain diggers to replace and imitate a lost convention.

PART 2

BITCOIN AND OTHER CRYPTOCURRENCIES

Today, Bitcoin is one of the most popular topics in the world of business, finances, economy and many other fields! If the current trends and forecasts are to be believed, then Bitcoin is here to stay – and not only stay; it's about to transform the world, unbelievably!

Learning about Bitcoin and everything it encompasses requires a basic start. So let us start with the very first question that comes to mind – what is it?

WHAT IS BITCOIN??

Developed and held electronically, Bitcoin is a type of digital currency. It is decentralized since no-one really controls it and transactions have no mediators; they are performed between two entities alone.

Representing a monetary unit, a Bitcoin is just a piece of a mathematical algorithm or a computer code. It is unique because Bitcoin is the first decentralized peer-to-peer network of payments that is supported by the users without any central authority, and is also referred to as Internet cash.

Though it has been created as a mining reward, digital currency can also be exchanged for products, other currencies and even some services in both black and legal markets. Bitcoin owners can also hold their coins as an investment for future profit generation.

WHAT IS CRYPTOCURRENCY?

Cryptocurrency is secure and anonymous digital money that has been designed using the Blockchain technology. Being available solely over the internet, it cannot be printed out as a tangible object. This currency, associated with the internet, uses cryptography- the process of converting legible information into a code that is almost impossible to crack.

Invented to resolve the need for secure communication since the Second World War, cryptography has evolved from the conventional elements of mathematical theory and computer science to become a digital way to secure communications, information and money online.

HOW DO CRYPTOCURRENCIES WORK?

Using decentralized technology, cryptocurrencies are digital money used for secure payments and money storage without the need to use names or visit a bank and are run on a distributed public ledger, which records all transactions spent and held by currency holders.

PART 2

Cryptocurrencies are created through a process called mining, which uses computer power to solve complicated numerical problems that generate coins as a reward for the miners. The currencies can also be bought from brokers, and then stored and spent using digital storages called cryptographic wallets.

Gaining momentum in the financial sectors, the potential of cryptocurrencies and Blockchain technology is quite huge and can be used for transactions including bonds, stocks and other financial assets.

WHAT ARE THE MOST COMMON CRYPTOCURRENCIES?

The internet hosts more than 900 cryptocurrencies that are still growing without any sign of slowing down, and this growth is mostly attributed to the success of Bitcoin, the value of which has increased manifold since its introduction. Bitcoin is without a doubt the largest Blockchain network, followed by Ethereum, Ripple then Litecoin – all by market capitalization. Let us delve into each of these cryptocurrencies one by one:

Bitcoin

Needing no introduction, Bitcoin is the first and the most commonly traded cryptocurrency today. Developed by an unknown entity called Satoshi Nakamoto in 2009, Bitcoin has a market capitalization of around $45 billion as of July 2017 and had increased to more than $66 billion by mid-August 2017. As of 14 August 2017 the value had already crossed the $4,000 mark, which is much more than solid gold. The price of Bitcoin was up more than 40% in August 2017, and more than 280% since the beginning of 2017.

Designed to have only 21 million coins in total, there are more than approximately $16 million Bitcoins in circulation which are all estimated to have been mined by 2040. Bitcoins can be divided into smaller units; the smallest is at one hundred millionth of a Bitcoin which is called a "Satoshi", named after the founder.

What Happens after all the Bitcoins are Mined?

Because of its finite supply, Bitcoin can either be celebrated by supporters or cautioned by sceptics. Bitcoin's fixed supply is favorable to most because it takes you back to the days of a sound gold standard. There are numerous similarities between Gold and Bitcoin, the most obvious one being their fixed supply. Gold must be extracted from the earth and put into circulation as market prices dictate. Bitcoin, if it ever achieves as widespread use as gold, can accomplish these same things with its own fixed supply.

The benefits of gold are taken a step further by Bitcoin with it being digital. The supply of Bitcoin not only incapacitates arbitrary manipulation but also eliminates the need for paper substitutes. Heavy and voluminous, gold is less preferable to many in comparison to paper substitutes. Gold thus remains stored in the bank, forcing people to trust the bank to handle their gold responsibly. Being tangible and handled by humans, there is a definite possibility for the gold to go missing from the bank. This issue is eliminated by the digital nature of Bitcoin since it costs almost nothing to store, and it takes up zero physical space in the real world. The best part is that it is globally intangible.

In spite of these wondrous benefits, there is still a lot of skepticism about the finite supply of Bitcoins. The behavior of miners, once all Bitcoins are mined, is the next worry. In an unsustainable mining system, once all the Bitcoins are out then miners will have to rely on transaction fees to keep themselves financially operational. Miner fees instead of a block reward will make mining very unaffordable to users, which will lead to miner shrinkage, centralization of the network and a possible collapse as well.

Ethereum

Ethereum is the second most widely-used and valuable cryptocurrency after Bitcoin. Developed in 2015 Ethereum has a market capitalization of around $18 billion as of July 2017, in spite of a stormy journey. After a major hack in 2016, it split into two currencies. Recently its value has reached a high of $400 but has also crashed briefly to as low as 10 cents.

Though being a distributed public Blockchain network similar to Bitcoin, there are a few significant technical differences which primarily show that Bitcoin and Ethereum are substantially different in their goals and capacity. Bitcoin offers a peer-to-peer electronic cash system for online Bitcoin payments which is one Blockchain application. The Bitcoin Blockchain can help with tracking digital currency ownership; the Ethereum Blockchain works on running the code of a decentralized application.

BLOCKCHAIN

In the Ethereum Blockchain, miners mine for Ether- a crypto token used to run the network. Apart from being a cryptocurrency that can be traded, application developers also use Ether to pay for transaction fees and services on the network.

The origin of Ethereum

Vitalik Buterin, a 19-year-old programmer from Toronto, was piqued by Bitcoin in 2011 and conceived a cryptocurrency from the idea of it.

Having co-founded the online news website Bitcoin Magazine in the same year and writing hundreds of articles on the cryptocurrency world, he coded for the Dark Wallet and the Egora market place.

During his research, he devised the idea of a platform that would go beyond the financial use of Bitcoin. Having written a white paper that described an alternate platform for any type of application that is decentralized that developers will want to build, he named the system Ethereum. Creating smart contracts and being a self-enforcing code that developers can tap for a range of applications, using Ethereum is easy.

What is a smart contract?

A smart contract is one that self-executes, handling the enforcement, the management, performance and payment - a smart contract lives up to its name. A computer code that can facilitate the exchange of money, content, property, shares or any value, it acts like a self-initiated program that auto-executes when certain conditions are met on the Blockchain. They run exactly as programmed without any censorship, downtime, fraud potential or third-party interference because of their base on the Blockchain.

Even though most code-processing Blockchains are limited, Ethereum is different. Instead of hosting limited operations, Ethereum allows the creation of desirable operations thus giving developers the ability to build thousands of different applications that go way beyond anything we have seen before.

The Ethereum Virtual Machine

Blockchain applications had their functional limitations before the creation of Ethereum. Initially, Bitcoin and the other cryptocurrencies were developed to operate as peer-to-peer digital currencies solely.

The issue that developers faced was that they were torn between either expanding the set of functions offered by Bitcoin and other applications, which was very complicated and time-consuming, or developing a new Blockchain application and an entirely new platform. Vitalik Buterin developed a new approach to creating Ethereum.

The EVM or the Ethereum Virtual Machine is the core innovation of Ethereum. EVM is a "complete Turing software" running on the Ethereum network. Allowing anyone to run any program, regardless of the programming language as long as there is enough time and memory, the Ethereum Virtual Machine eases the process of creating Blockchain applications thus making it more efficient than ever before. Reducing effort by not needing to design a completely original Blockchain for every new application, Ethereum helps with the development of innumerable different applications on a single platform.

Ethereum looks more capable than Bitcoin – this is based purely on the impact that it is expected to create, in spite of having a much lower value as of August 2017. Ethereum could open a whole new era of possibilities in the future.

Ripple

Founded in 2012, Ripple is another distributed ledger system that can be used to track more types of transactions than just cryptocurrencies. Used by banks like Santander and UBS, it has a market value of around $6.3 billion.

Ripple addresses the need to keep money flowing freely, as conveyed by its parent company OpenCoin. Ripple has the following goals:

• Building on the decentralized digital currency approach which already has been laid out by Bitcoin.

• Replicate what the Internet did for all forms of information, but with money.

Similarities between Ripple and the Internet

Today's cash systems can be compared to the Internet in the 80's. Back then every provider built their own system for their customers, and people using different systems couldn't easily interact with each other effectively. Designed to connect different payment systems together, the network that Ripple uses allows effortless transfer of any form of currency, regardless of country.

Similar to Bitcoin, the XRP unit of Ripple is digital and based on mathematical calculations that have a limit on the number of units to be mined. Transferrable from account to account, both these currencies can do without an intermediary bank and provide digital security to guard against the possibility of fake coins.

Ripple and Bitcoin complement each other very well. Enabling connections between Bitcoin and those using other currencies, expedited transactions and increased stability are offered by Ripple. Ripple does not depend on a single company to manage and secure the transaction database, being a distributed network. Also block confirmations require zero waiting, thus enabling fast transaction confirmations through the network.

How many Ripples will there be?

The target is to create 100 billion Ripples. OpenCoin will release half of those in circulation, while it will retain the other half.

Although it doesn't receive transaction fees like PayPal, banks and credit cards, it does take a tiny portion of a Ripple, equivalent to ~1/1000th of a cent from each transaction. The amount collected is destroyed rather than retained, since this deduction is to safeguard against the system being tricked by an entity trying to put through millions of transactions through simultaneously.

Litecoin

Being most similar to Bitcoin, LiteCoin has quickly innovated techniques of faster payments and processes to allow more transactions. The total value of Litecoin is around $2.1 billion as of August 2017.

BLOCKCHAIN

Bitcoin, being an open source code and the world's first cryptocurrency developed by Satoshi Nakamoto, turned out to be an inspiration for many developers. Many cryptocurrencies in the market are mostly modified versions of this code, with varying levels of success.

Announced in 2011, the makers of Litecoin wanted it to be the 'silver' to Bitcoin's 'gold'. At this juncture, Litecoin has the highest market cap of any mined cryptocurrency after Bitcoin.

Generated through mining, Litecoin was created by Charles Lee who is a former Google engineer. Having seen flaws in Bitcoin, Charles was motivated to improve on that technology - thus creating Litecoin. The block generation time is the major factor differentiating Litecoin from Bitcoin. Bitcoin requires 10 minutes in comparison to Litecoin's 2.5 minutes to generate a block. Having faster transaction confirmation time compared to Bitcoin, there are several implications to it listed below:

• Due to a faster block generation rate, Litecoin can handle a much higher volume of transactions. Bitcoin would require a significant number of updates to the code that everyone on the Bitcoin network was currently running to match up to this speed. As an example, a merchant who waited for a minimum of two confirmations would only need to wait 5 minutes with Litecoin, whereas they would have to wait 10 minutes for just one confirmation with Bitcoin. This shows that Litecoin's block generation is four times faster than Bitcoin's.

• The Litecoin Blockchain will be proportionately larger than Bitcoin's, with more orphaned blocks, as a result of a higher number of blocks which is a disadvantage.

• The risk of double spending attacks is reduced due to the faster block time of Litecoin– this is theoretical in the case of both networks having the same hashing power.

• Many involved with Bitcoin often do not regard transaction speed (or faster block time) and confirmation speed as a factor to consider, because most merchants allow zero-confirmation transactions for purchases. An important point is that a transaction is immediate and it is just confirmed by the network as it propagates.

• From a more technical perspective Litecoin and Bitcoin differ in a more important factor, which is the proof of work algorithm. Bitcoin uses the SHA-256 hashing algorithm, which involves calculations that can be greatly accelerated in parallel processing. Bitcoin's difficulty level has greatly increased because of this characteristic that has given rise to the intense race in ASIC technology.

• Litecoin uses the scrypt algorithm (pronounced as 'script'). This algorithm, though it incorporates SHA-256, performs calculations that are much more serialized than those of SHA256 in Bitcoin. Scrypt requires large amounts of high-speed RAM rather than raw processing power.

WHY WOULD YOU USE A CRYPTOCURRENCY?

Being secure and providing a level of anonymity, transactions in cryptocurrencies cannot be faked or reversed and the fees for them are much lower, making it a more trusted medium than conventional currency. Since they are decentralized they are open to everyone, whereas banks can be exclusive when it comes to who they will want to deal with.

As a new form of cash, the cryptocurrency markets are popular for those believing that a small investment can become a large sum overnight. True stories of millionaires created through an investment of Bitcoin have become famous. But the same can work the other way. Due to the high risks involved the market of cryptocurrencies is highly volatile. Because of this, people who are looking to invest in cryptocurrencies should exercise caution before they get involved, although this investment is better than the lottery and stock market.

SMART CONTRACTS

WHAT IS A 'SMART CONTRACT'?

In layman terms, 'smart contract' could refer to any agreement which executes itself when the terms between the entities are encoded within its code.

The code of smart contracts can be run on a computer and can set strict rules along with the consequences in a way similar to that of a customary legal paper, stating the responsibilities, benefits and penalties which are to be abided by both parties under various conditions. Unlike a traditional contract, it can furthermore take the information as an input and process that over the terms of the agreement, and take any actions as an outcome.

WHY USE SMART CONTRACTS?

Allowing users to trade and conduct business with outsiders over the internet, without any intermediary, is the foremost purpose of designing smart contracts. Trust and its elements are the most significant factors when shopping online, hiring resources over the internet and conducting trade with outsiders over the internet.

TYPES AND INSTANCES OF SMART CONTRACT

Avoiding breaches: One of the earliest and simplest instances of a smart contract is Digital Privileges Management or DRM technologies. This kind of contract does not take or process inputs, however simply imposes itself by making it impossible for you to unofficially break the contract. An example would be breaking a contract by copying music or a video file which is secured by copyright.

Property Decree: Cryptocurrencies like Bitcoin can be defined as a set of smart contracts which implement the law of property. Cryptographic methods are used to ensure that only the proprietor of a digital token like Bitcoin can spend it. Numerous dispersed asset exchanges exist, which widen out the variety of assets so that many diverse digital assets can be traded on any distinct Blockchain. A similar principle can also be protracted to physical products by electronic panels or entrenched microchips.

Financial Service: Cryptocurrency clearly opens up an extensive range of diverse use cases for smart contracts which would not otherwise be probable.

Credit Enforcement: An addition to the law of property, as well as a classic instance of how smart contracts could be used in the actual world, is credit contracts which deactivate your product if you fail to make your repayments.

Oracle Contracts: The primary limitation of smart contracts is that a computer program cannot simply and reliably tell what is occurring in the physical world.

Double Deposit Technique: Initially, smart contracts in the empire of cryptocurrency used the dual deposit method initiated by BitHalo and BlackHalo. This simple, but still very potent technique is preferably used with cryptocurrency.

BITCOIN AND BUSINESS

The way we do business today is slowly and gradually changing because of Bitcoin, and it is both a secure and inexpensive manner of handling payments.

Here are some of many reasons that make Bitcoin ideal for business:

- No Fee. Since there is no fee for receiving Bitcoins, we can choose our fee. It is also important to mention that fees aren't only related to the amount of money in transactions and many wallets allow control over the sum to pay when spending.

PART 2

- No frauds. Since payments made in Bitcoins are secure and irreversible, the costs of frauds don't result in costing customers money. PayPal and credit card payments do penalize customers for these unfortunate scenarios.

- International payments. For success in business, it is important to consider the entire world as one big market and try to reach that global market. That being said international payments can be quite complicated and transfer money via banks requires 3-5 business days, without considering any other limitations and obstacles. Bitcoin is different and makes international payments significantly easier, which is what every business owner desires.

- PCI compliance isn't required. Securing the wallet and payment requests is required by Bitcoin, but users don't need to carry the costs and responsibilities associated with sensitive information like credit card numbers. Similarly, businesses that accept credit cards online need to go through extensive security checks and comply with PCI standards

- Marketing. One of the most practical moves for online businesses is accepting a new payment method. The success of any business, big or small, depends on their market worth, which Bitcoin can also help with. Accepting Bitcoins shows that a business keeps up with the latest trends and adapts to them quickly. This is a great way to get more visibility and is a smart marketing strategy.

49

- Multi-signature option. This allows Bitcoins to be spent only if a transaction is authorized or approved by a group of entities. This is useful when a business or company has a board of directors because it prevents unlawful activities and one person isn't able to spend outrageous sums of money without it getting approved.

- Transparency. Bitcoin increases transparency, which is vital in business. The entire process allows you to provide information that members can use to verify transactions and balances. Even non-profit organizations can benefit from Bitcoin because, that way, their donations are public.

WHY START ACCEPTING BITCOINS?

Are you a business owner? If so, accepting Bitcoins should be your next primary goal. Digital currencies are the future of business payments, and being on the forefront will definitely put your company on the grid and make it unique. On an obvious note, this attracts a whole new group of people. Besides the benefits of Bitcoins listed above, here are other reasons to accept these digital coins:

- Near-instant settlement of payments

- Faster access to money

- Decreased liability for customer data, meaning the recipient needs to know almost nothing about the sender of the payment

- Accepting Bitcoins empowers customers

PART 2

- The support from the Bitcoin Community leads to improved business

- Increased brand awareness

- An opportunity to become or join industry leaders

- You don't have to be an expert in Bitcoins to start accepting them

- No chargebacks or returns

Let us now enlist the benefits of paying with Bitcoins:

- Discretion – unless a user publishes his/her Bitcoin transactions voluntarily, their purchases aren't linked to their personal identity

- No intermediaries or third-party interruptions

- Purchases are free of sales tax

- Transaction fee is very low

- Get online and pay – you only need an internet connection

SOME OF THE COMPANIES THAT ACCEPT BITCOIN

Living in the digital age would definitely include digital currencies at some point in time. Now, we have Bitcoins and some other cryptocurrencies inspired by them. The more popular they get, the more their value rises, and it comes as no surprise that many businesses have decided to accept Bitcoin. Here is a list featuring some of the many companies that allow their customers to pay with Bitcoin: *Apple, Dell Inc., Dish, eBay, eGifter, Etsy, Expedia, Foodler, Intuit, Lions Gate Entertainment, Microsoft Corporation, Newegg, Overstock.com, PayPal Shopify stores, Square Inc., Starbucks, Tesla, Time and Zynga Inc.*

International payments

Bitcoin is ideal and immensely popular for international payments. Taking too long (3-5 days) and having to pay outrageously high fees are the major drawbacks of the conventional payment systems that exist today. Both of these factors are true in most cases, and both the sender and the recipient do not have much privacy given that they have to share all their information.

Using cutting-edge, innovative technology to design new types of payment architecture, Bitcoins have private keys that are at the disposal of every user. When a payment needs to be made, wallets that hold the Bitcoins will help you to send the amount to the recipient directly.

Bitcoin is the ideal tool to use if you are against the paying of high fees and don't want transfers to take 3-5 business days. It allows users to purchase goods and services or send payments across the border, wherever this cryptocurrency is accepted, without the need for an intermediary who takes a commission.

The entire process of initiating to validating a transaction takes about 10 minutes with Bitcoin. Due to the advanced value of international payments with Bitcoin, many intermediaries and central banks are evaluating the technology used for this purpose to find out if adopting those technologies and implementing them could improve the security and timeliness of their own international payment systems.

Safe, confidential and fast payments are the prime benefits of Bitcoin and are important for everyone, especially business owners. Selling and purchasing with Bitcoins eliminates the necessity of managing multiple currency accounts.

Purchasing Bitcoins online can be done using payment services like PayPal or bank transfer. Acquiring the Bitcoin equivalent of the amount you'd like to send internationally, you can send the Bitcoins directly to the recipient. Of course, you are not obliged to purchase Bitcoins if you already own them or if you engage in Bitcoin mining.

WHAT IS BITCOIN MINING?

Bitcoin Mining is an important aspect of the Bitcoin world and requires thorough analysis which is why we have dedicated this chapter to it.

What is Bitcoin mining?

The definition of Bitcoin mining describes it as a peer-to-peer computer process that is used to verify and secure Bitcoin payments or transactions from one user to another. With an objective of securing the transactions recorded in the public ledger or Blockchain of Bitcoin, it can also serve to release new Bitcoins.

Cryptography enthusiasts, individuals passionate about revolutionizing digital currencies and others who were interested in the entire process were the original Bitcoin miners. Recognizing the business opportunity in Bitcoin mining, once the value of Bitcoin skyrocketed investors started investing in hardware and warehouses. As a result it became difficult for interested parties to keep up with this process, but there are still some miners who do it as a hobby.

Bitcoin mining can be compared to gold mining in some ways. There are only a limited number of Bitcoins (21 million). The more Bitcoins that are found and taken out then the more grueling it becomes to get more, simultaneously increasing their value.

Bitcoins are a sort of reward for miners when they validate transactions and the network compensates them by releasing these digital coins for contributing with the necessary computational power.

Naturally the more computing power a person contributes, the greater the reward. Requiring special programs and high-end computers, miners use the computer resources and the program to compete with each other and strive to solve complex mathematical problems.

Ten minutes is the average time that is taken to solve a block containing the latest transaction data by miners, with the help of cryptographic hash functions.

How is Bitcoin mining done?

Let's delve into the actual mining process with the requirements detailed below:

PART 2

- Hardware

    Adequate hardware is a prerequisite to Bitcoin Mining. Initially, miners needed only their computer's high speed video processor card or CPU. Now with the advent of newer technology, custom Bitcoin ASIC chips offer performance which is 100 times greater than the capability of the older systems, which older versions of computer hardware wouldn't be able to endure. Inadequate hardware consumes more energy than you earn- which minimizes or totally removes the profit margin. Let us get a basic rundown of good and bad hardware options for Bitcoin mining:

    - CPU – This outdated hardware was the ideal option back in the initial phases of Bitcoin, but now it doesn't have the strength and potential equivalent to the energy it consumes. You could mine for decades without earning a single coin.

    - GPU – GPU hardware gradually replaced the slow and inefficient CPU about a year and a half after the commencement of Bitcoin mining. GPU took credit for 50x-100x increase in Bitcoin mining power while using a reduced level of power per unit of work. Any modern GPU can be utilized for Bitcoin mining; the AMD line is way superior to Nvidia, with the ATI Radeon HD 5870 being the most efficient option (at the time of writing).

    - FPGA (Field Programmable Gate Array) – Its ease of use and efficient power consumption made this hardware extremely handy even though it didn't allow a 50x-100x increase in Bitcoin mining.

- ASIC – Today, Bitcoin mining is in the era of ASIC (Application Specific Integrated Circuit), which is just a chip created with the purpose of performing only a single task. It cannot be repurposed to do another function, which means that an ASIC that is designed for Bitcoin mining can only mine these coins with the sole benefit being preserving more power.

People who don't have the required hardware use cloud mining services that make things easier, but the since miners have no control over the hardware there is a chance of the risks outweighing the benefits.

- Software

Special software is also needed for Bitcoin mining in addition to excellent hardware. Many downloadable programs, the most popular ones being BFGminer and CGminer, are available - both of which are command line programs.

- Mining Pool

Being a part of a Bitcoin mining pool or mining on your own are the two ways to implement Bitcoin mining. Most miners prefer pooling because the luck is naturally higher, though when mining in the pool all profit you generate is divided among the members. In contrast, when mining on your own, the profit is all yours, but the profit generation could obviously take longer!

PART 2

- Bitcoin Wallet

    Creating a Bitcoin wallet before you join a pool is a good practice since a wallet holds your Bitcoins just like your "regular" wallet holds your money.

    Securing Bitcoin from potential danger and threats, the Bitcoin wallet offers a two-factor authentication. Keeping your Bitcoin wallet on an offline computer without internet access is another secure option. A Bitcoin Wallet can be obtained by downloading a software client to the computer.

- Electricity cost

    The cost of electricity is an important concern for the mining process, which has the primary operational costs of electricity and hardware, both for providing proper ventilation and cooling and running the miners.

    While mining does require more power and energy, it can be cleverly maintained by having Bitcoin mining operations located close to a cheap electricity supply.

    North America's largest mining operation, regulated by MegaBigPower, is situated by the Columbia River, Washington State since hydroelectric power is abundant here and prices are the cheapest in the country. Additionally a large mining operation in Iceland, run by CloudHashing, is cheap and renewable due to hydroelectric and geothermal power sources, with the cold climate characteristic of northern Europe providing the much-needed cooling.

57

- Regulation - Tax guidance was issued by the IRS wherein they announced that income generated from Bitcoin mining constituted self-employment income and should be subjected to tax. Today there are no specific and strict regulations regarding Bitcoin mining, but seeing that the value of Bitcoin is getting stronger by the day a number of guidelines are bound to be created.

WHAT IS PROOF OF WORK?

A proof of work is a term frequently mentioned in Bitcoin mining world, referring to a piece of data which was expensive, time-consuming or difficult to produce to meet certain criteria. In order to be considered valid individual blocks need to contain some proof of work, which has to be verified by other Bitcoin nodes each time a block is received. In addition, Bitcoin also uses proof of work to prevent double-spending.

IS BITCOIN SECURE?

The internet opens a wide door to possibilities and opportunities which bring along an equal amount of risk and danger with them. With digital currencies it is always important to identity thefts, hacks and many other unfortunate scenarios. The same applies for Bitcoin as well since it is a currency generated and used online. Let us look into the safety aspect of Bitcoin and what can be done to make it more secure.

PART 2

BITCOIN SECURITY

Having a very strong security track record, the Bitcoin technology boasts of its incredible safety being its biggest advantage and its vulnerabilities mostly being user errors.

Though being one of the safest methods to use and send payments, different security flaws have been recorded throughout the history of Bitcoin but these were always identified and fixed promptly.

Bitcoin's security, as with any software, depends on the speed of discovery and fixing the security flaws. The more quickly the problems are identified, the safer the currency is.

Here are some interesting facts about security flaws on Bitcoin:

1. Most Bitcoin thefts are the consequence of mismanaged or inadequate wallet security

2. 1 in every 16/17 Bitcoins belonging to someone was stolen

3. An approximate value of stolen Bitcoins since 2009 is $500 million

With irreversible payments being irreversible and the recipient approval being the only way to get a refund, this can be advantageous to hackers to exploit vulnerabilities within wallets to steal Bitcoins. One Reddit user claimed that someone transferred about $70,000 worth of Bitcoins to their account without his authorization.

BLOCKCHAIN

In spite of a history of different hacks and security flaws, compared to the number of transactions and payments and to the number of Bitcoin users it is safe to conclude these security mishaps are very rare.

Saying that a security flaw makes Bitcoin unsafe is equivalent to saying that a bank being robbed compromises the dollar, which is not the case. Today, the Blockchain architecture is immune to hacking attacks since hacking into Bitcoin would require considerable computing power.

Intuitive or user-friendly security solutions and an entire set of ethical or good practices are being conceived regularly to reduce fraud and protect money better by Bitcoin developers. This has resulted in Bitcoin developing numerous security features, including hardware wallets, offline wallets, wallet encryption, multi-signature transactions and many other security strategies.

HOW CAN YOU PROTECT YOUR BITCOIN?

Though it is still one of the safest and easiest ways to make payments and transactions, the Bitcoin wallet is prone to mismanagement and to consumers failing to secure their profiles adequately. Minimize security flaws with these tips:

- Avoid storing your Private Key and wallet address in the same place

- Use only your PC or phone to make transactions

- Use multiple wallets such as desktop, mobile and offline

- Backup your wallet on offline hard drive(s)

PART 2

- Use third-party encryption

Securing the wallet

Keeping your wallet safe and protected is of the utmost importance since it contains your Bitcoins. Ensuring your wallet is secure and keeping security flaws at bay necessary. The steps below will help you do this:

1. Be careful with storing money with an online service and don't any website's security for granted, since websites are prone to different security breaches.

2. Use two-factor authentication.

3. Only small amounts of Bitcoins should be kept on a phone, computer or server as running money, with the remainder stowed away in a safer environment.

4. Backup your wallet to protect your Bitcoin from human mistakes and computer failures

5. Encrypt the wallet or smartphone by setting the password to protect against misuse

6. A cold wallet i.e. an offline wallet provides the highest level of security for Bitcoin saving, which means storing a wallet in a safe and secure place that isn't connected to the internet.

7. Keep the Bitcoin software up to date in order to receive security and stability updates. Updates come with new, useful features that only add to the overall security of your wallet.

BLOCKCHAIN

8. Using a multi-signature option is advisable if more than person has access to the Bitcoin account.

So, be safe and protect yourself and the Bitcoins online by keeping a track of the market, learning how it works and being cautious with all online services.

CONCLUSION

There is a lot more to Bitcoins and Blockchains than their use as an exchange for currency for online shopping. Hopefully, this book has opened the realm of possibilities that are available to those that choose to pursue them.

Despite the fact that the technology seems to be perfect for all those who are involved in finance, it is evident that it is applicable to many other domains and industries. For the moment Blockchain technology seems like an interruption to the status quo, though that is how most new technologies are seen before they are finally accepted for what they are. Let us open our minds to the future, and embrace this technology that is here to stay, and is here to change our lives for the better.

www.ingramcontent.com/pod-product-compliance
Lightning Source LLC
Chambersburg PA
CBHW070217230526
45471CB00002B/967